THE *VOYAGER* SPACE PROBES

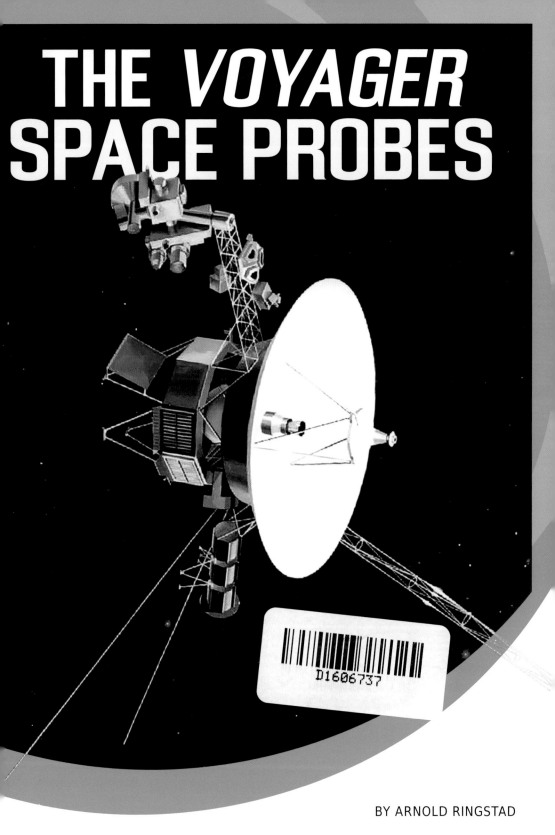

D1606737

BY ARNOLD RINGSTAD

Published by The Child's World®
1980 Lookout Drive • Mankato, MN 56003-1705
800-599-READ • www.childsworld.com

Acknowledgments
The Child's World®: Mary Berendes, Publishing Director
Red Line Editorial: Design, editorial direction, and production
Photographs ©: Photographs ©: NASA, cover, 1, 8, 11, 12, 14, 16, 19, 21, 23; AP
Images, 4; Red Line Editorial, 7; Corbis, 15

ISBN 9781634074803

LCCN 2015946222

Printed in the United States of America
Mankato, MN
December, 2015
PA02280

ABOUT THE AUTHOR

Arnold Ringstad is the author of more than 30 books for kids. He loves
reading and writing about space exploration. He lives in Minnesota.

TABLE OF CONTENTS

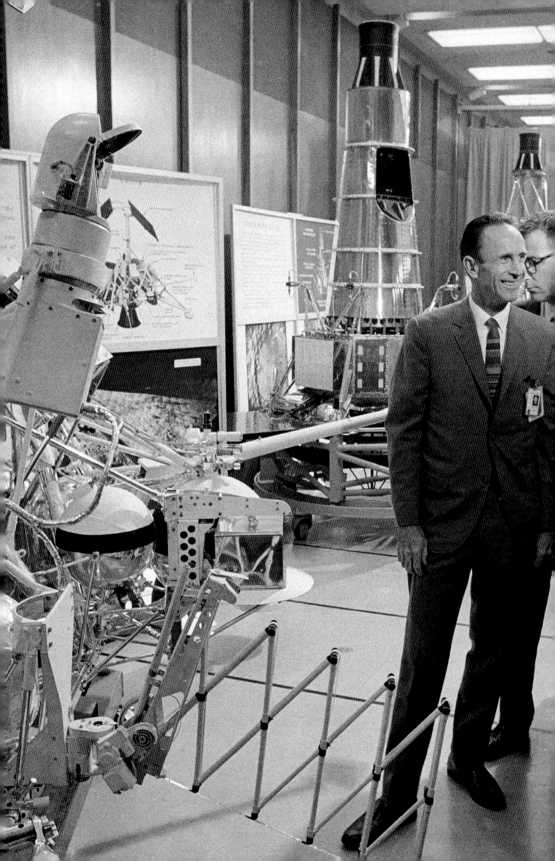

Chapter 1

A GRAND TOUR

On a hot summer day in 1965, Gary Flandro looked at his graph paper and thought hard. Flandro was a college student. He was also a part-time worker at the Jet Propulsion Laboratory (JPL). The JPL is a government research center that explores space with unmanned spacecraft. Earlier that year, Flandro had received a new assignment from his JPL bosses. He would be studying possible new space exploration missions.

Flandro was interested in sending ships to the outer solar system. This includes the planets Jupiter, Saturn, Uranus, and Neptune. All four are large planets made up mostly of whirling, flowing gases. Flandro knew a spacecraft visiting these worlds would send back valuable information. But there was one problem. These planets were amazingly far away.

◄ A group tours the Jet Propulsion Laboratory in the late 1960s.

Sending a ship straight to Neptune would take 40 years. Flandro would be ready to retire by the time it got there. He wondered if there was a faster way.

Flying to another planet is difficult. Knowing the planet's current location is not enough. Scientists have to know where the planet will be when the spacecraft gets there. Flandro scribbled on his graph paper. He sketched out the motion of the planets years into the future. He began to notice something interesting.

In the 1970s, the gas giants would line up. A ship could fly near Jupiter. Then it could use the planet's **gravity** to slingshot toward Saturn. The ship could do the same thing to visit Uranus and Neptune. The spacecraft would reach Neptune in only eight years.

Flandro showed the plan to his bosses at JPL. They were excited about the mission. It was nicknamed the Planetary Grand Tour. But they knew it would be challenging. Eight years was much longer than previous space missions. One engineer told Flandro, "We can't build a spacecraft that will last over two years, let alone eight years!"[1]

Communicating with the spacecraft would be hard, too. Engineers did not know if a spacecraft so far away could send signals back to Earth. They also worried about intense **radiation** near Jupiter. It could damage equipment and make the spacecraft useless.

The launch was planned for 1977. That meant scientists had about ten years to solve these problems.

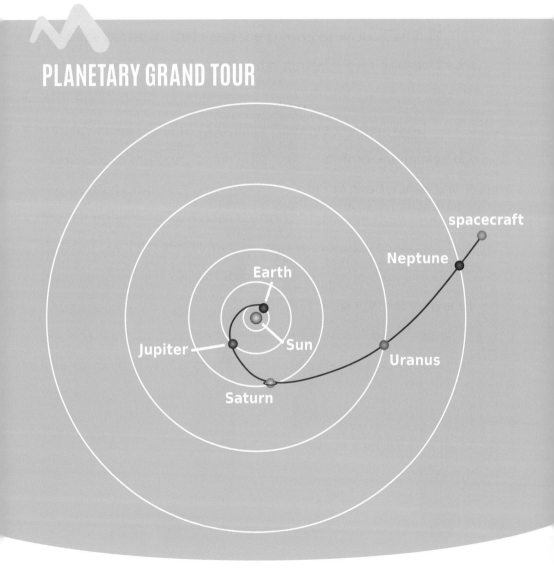

PLANETARY GRAND TOUR

spacecraft

Neptune

Earth

Jupiter — Sun

Uranus

Saturn

Chapter 2

PREPARING TO LAUNCH

A different spacecraft, the *Pioneer 10*, sped toward Jupiter in the fall of 1973. It was not part of the Grand Tour. Even so, engineers watched it nervously. No ship had ever been to Jupiter before. *Pioneer 10* would send back data. The Grand Tour engineers could use that information in the design of their own ship. It would tell them how dangerous Jupiter's radiation really was.

When the data came in, the team was shocked. The radiation was much worse than they had expected. The engineers worked throughout 1974 to fix their ship. They added shielding to protect sensitive computers and sensors.

Mission planners decided there would be two identical ships. They would be called *Voyager 1* and *Voyager 2*. Both would launch in 1977. Before they blasted off, astronomer Carl Sagan

◄ *Voyager 2* **blasts off from Kennedy Space Center in 1977.**

added one last thing to them. Sagan knew the *Voyager* ships would leave the solar system. They would be the first ships from Earth to travel so far. Sagan wanted to include a message from their home planet. If living beings ever found the spacecraft, they could learn about the planet it came from.

The message was on a gold disc. It was packed with information. It had images of everyday life on Earth. It also had recorded greetings in many languages. It had music, animal noises, and many other sounds. It even showed where Earth is located. Two of these gold discs were made. Engineers bolted them onto the *Voyager* spacecraft. Soon, it would be time to send them into space.

On August 20, 1977, *Voyager 2* sat atop a massive Titan IIIE rocket. It would be the first of the twin spaceships to leave Earth. The rocket roared to life, carrying *Voyager 2* into the sky. The ship reached space safely and began its long trip to Jupiter. *Voyager 1* launched two weeks later on September 5. The two spacecraft took different paths. This meant *Voyager 1* would arrive at Jupiter first. Gary Flandro's graph paper plans had become reality. It was time for the Grand Tour to begin.

The gold disc (top) and its cover (bottom) could someday help ▶ other living beings understand life on Earth.

Chapter 3

JUPITER AND SATURN

Voyager 1 approached Jupiter in the spring of 1979. Scientists waited anxiously. Photos showed up on screens at mission control. Data from the spacecraft poured in. Scientists discovered Jupiter had rings. For the first time, scientists had clear views of Jupiter's moons. Ganymede, the largest moon in the solar system, was covered in **craters** and grooves. Callisto had craters, too. They were gigantic and faded. But the most exciting discovery came from the moon Io.

As it left Jupiter, *Voyager 1* took a photo of Io. Back on Earth, science team member Linda Morabito processed the image. She noticed something strange about it. Io had no **atmosphere**. But there was a cloud rising from its surface. Scientists gathered to discuss what it could be. They determined it was a volcanic eruption. It was the first active volcano ever seen outside of Earth.

◀ *Voyager 1* **took a picture that shows the Great Red Spot, a huge storm on Jupiter.**

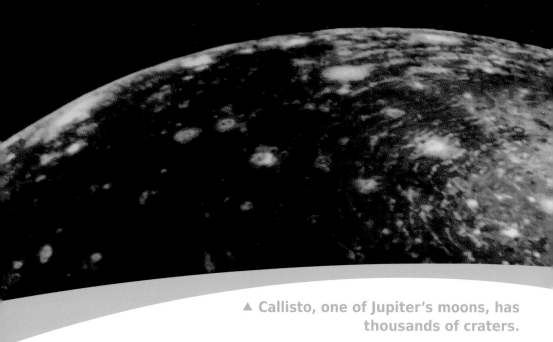

▲ Callisto, one of Jupiter's moons, has thousands of craters.

In July 1979, *Voyager 2* reached Jupiter. It discovered a new moon near Jupiter's rings. Scientists named it Adrastea. As *Voyager 2* zoomed around Jupiter, the huge planet's gravity grabbed the probe. It fired the spacecraft toward Saturn at 45,000 miles per hour (73,000 km/h).

More than a year later, the Grand Tour continued at Saturn. *Voyager 1* arrived first in November 1980. It sent back stunning images of Saturn's moons. Tethys had one of the solar system's longest valleys. Photos showed Iapetus to be half black and half white. Mimas had a gigantic crater. The spacecraft also studied Saturn itself. It took close-up photos of the planet's rings. But *Voyager 1*'s next target would be its last.

The spacecraft flew toward Saturn's moon Titan. Yellow clouds swirled in the moon's atmosphere. They made it impossible to see the surface. Some scientists had hoped life might exist below the cloud tops. But the moon remained mysterious.

Visiting Titan brought *Voyager 1*'s journey to an end. The moon's gravity flung the spacecraft on a path upward and out of the solar system. It would not be able to explore Uranus and Neptune. But its twin would continue where it had left off.

Voyager 2 zipped past Saturn in the summer of 1981. Uranus was more than four years away. The team on Earth spent the time carefully preparing for the next part of the Grand Tour.

▲ Saturn has many moons. They look like tiny dots compared to the huge planet.

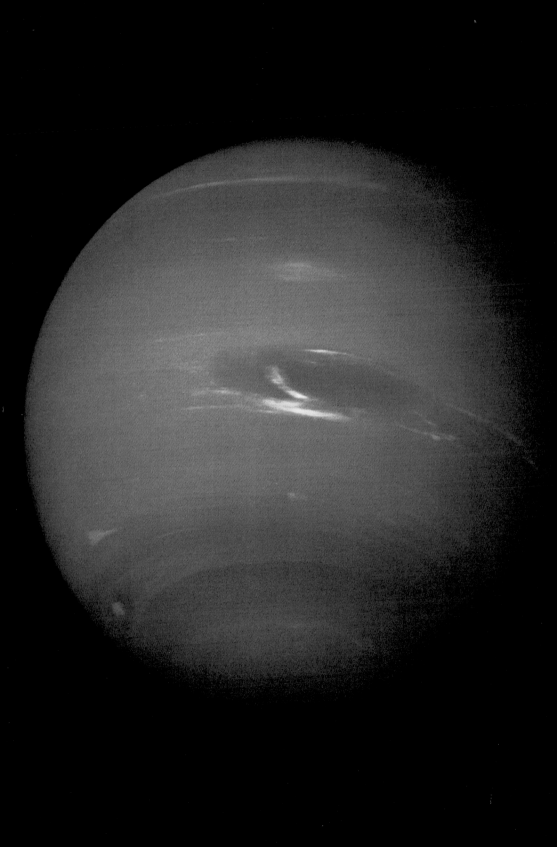

Chapter 4

CONTINUING ONWARD

Scientists knew much about Jupiter and Saturn before the *Voyager* spacecraft visited the planets. They could clearly see the great gas giants through telescopes. But Uranus and Neptune were different. Scientists knew little about these faraway blue planets. After an eight-year journey, *Voyager 2* would have only six hours to closely study Uranus. The scientists worked hard to make those hours count.

Voyager 2 approached Uranus in January 1986. The spacecraft worked quickly as it sped past the giant light-blue planet. It carried out more than 90 science experiments. It snapped photos with its camera. Tiny pieces of the planet's rings struck the spacecraft as it zoomed past. But *Voyager 2* kept working.

It took days for the spacecraft to beam back its data. Scientists studied the results. They were amazed. *Voyager 2* had discovered ten new moons around Uranus. The spacecraft had measured

◄ Neptune's blue appearance is caused in part by a gas called methane.

chemicals in the planet's atmosphere. It had mapped the planet's **magnetic field**, too. The team was proud of its spacecraft. After many years, it was still going strong. But another long wait lay ahead. *Voyager 2* cruised for 43 months through the cold, empty space of the outer solar system.

In August 1989, *Voyager 2* finally reached Neptune. The giant dark-blue planet loomed large in the spacecraft's camera. *Voyager 2* studied Neptune's whipping winds. It took photos of the planet's faint rings. It measured the planet's magnetic field. Finally, it headed for Neptune's moon Triton. This moon is the coldest known place in the solar system. Scientists saw gas erupting from Triton's surface. Clouds of nitrogen shot hundreds of miles into space.

Triton's gravity flung *Voyager 2* downward and out of the solar system. The ship floated silently away from Neptune. The huge blue planet shrank in *Voyager 2*'s view until it was just another bright spot among the stars. Both spacecraft had left the planets and moons of the solar system behind. But their missions were not yet over.

By early 1990, scientists had decided to turn off *Voyager 1*'s camera. There was little to see so far out in space. But Carl Sagan argued for one last photo. He said the ship had a unique

Neptune's moon Triton has geysers that erupt. ▶

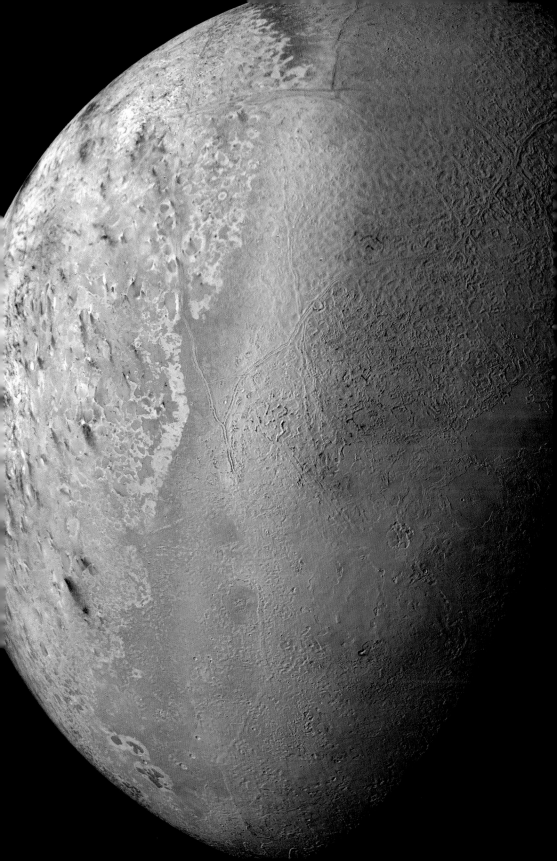

opportunity to see the whole solar system at once. The mission team agreed. On Valentine's Day of 1990, *Voyager 1* spun around. It pointed its camera toward home. Earth appeared as a tiny blue dot in a sea of blackness. The spacecraft was now more than 4 billion miles (6 billion km) away.

After this photo, the camera was shut down for good. Both *Voyager* spacecraft drifted through the darkness. Their final mission would be to study the edges of the solar system. This new journey was called the Voyager Interstellar Mission.

Voyager 1 was farther away than its twin. It would leave the solar system first. Scientists watched carefully for clues that the edge was near. Hints began to appear in 2012. *Voyager 1* beamed back unusual data. The number of particles it measured from the sun began dropping. Radiation coming from outside the solar system increased.

Measuring the **plasma** around *Voyager 1* would provide extra evidence. But the spacecraft's plasma sensor broke down in 1980. The scientists figured out a clever solution. A powerful **solar flare** might shake *Voyager 1*'s antennas. They could measure how the plasma vibrated. This would show the amount of plasma. But solar flares are rare. So scientists waited for a chance to test the solution.

▲ An artist's concept of *Voyager 1* leaving the solar system

Finally, a solar flare roared through space in early 2013. It struck *Voyager 1*. The ship sent back measurements. The data was clear. The spacecraft had left the solar system. More than 12,000 days after launch, *Voyager 1* was leaving home. It was on its way to the stars.

By 2015, both *Voyager* spacecraft still sent data back to Earth. Their power would last until at least 2020. After the power runs out, the twin ships will go silent. They will continue drifting through space forever. They will remain Earth's most distant travelers.

GLOSSARY

atmosphere (AT-mus-feer): An atmosphere is the layer of air that surrounds a planet. Saturn's moon Titan has a hazy atmosphere.

craters (KRAY-turz): Craters are bowl-shaped pits formed when a rock in space collides with a planet or moon. Jupiter's moon Ganymede has many craters.

gravity (GRAV-i-tee): Gravity is the force that pulls things together. Jupiter's powerful gravity boosted the *Voyager* spacecraft through the outer solar system.

magnetic field (mayg-NET-ik FEELD): A magnetic field is an area around powerful magnets where their magnetism can affect nearby objects. The *Voyager* spacecraft measured the magnetic field of Neptune and other planets and moons.

plasma (PLAZ-muh): Plasma is a gas that has changed and has new properties, such as sensitivity to magnetic fields. *Voyager 1* measured plasma to determine whether the spacecraft had left the solar system.

radiation (RAY-dee-AY-shun): Radiation is energy that is often invisible and can damage living things. Powerful radiation near Jupiter can harm spacecraft.

solar flare (SOL-ur FLAIR): A solar flare is a large burst of energy from the sun. A solar flare made it possible for *Voyager 1* to measure plasma in deep space.

SOURCE NOTES

1. Jay Gallentine. *Ambassadors from Earth: Pioneering Explorations with Unmanned Spacecraft.* Lincoln, NE: University of Nebraska Press, 2009. Print. 284.

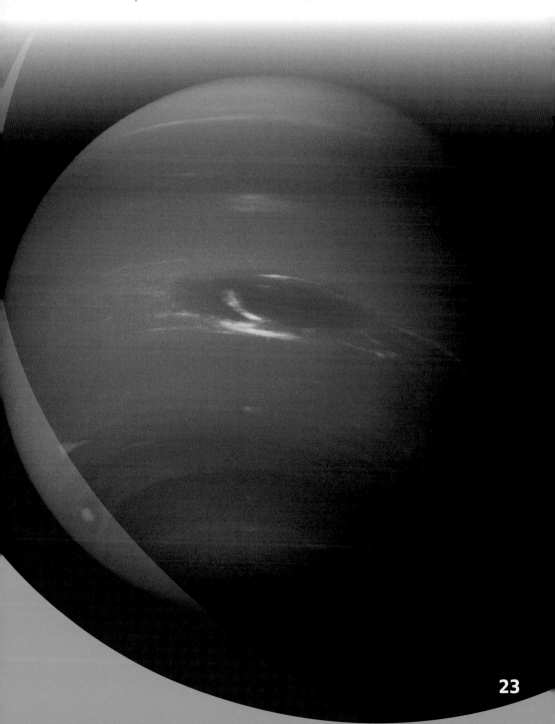

TO LEARN MORE

Books

Aguilar, David A. *Space Encyclopedia: A Tour of Our Solar System and Beyond*. Washington, DC: National Geographic Children's Books, 2013.

Owens, L. L. *Jupiter*. Mankato, MN: Child's World, 2011.

Owens, L. L. *Saturn*. Mankato, MN: Child's World, 2011.

Web Sites

Visit our Web site for links about the *Voyager* space probes: childsworld.com/links

Note to Parents, Teachers, and Librarians: We routinely verify our Web links to make sure they are safe and active sites. So encourage your readers to check them out!

INDEX